Healthy Hands and Feet

Constance Milburn

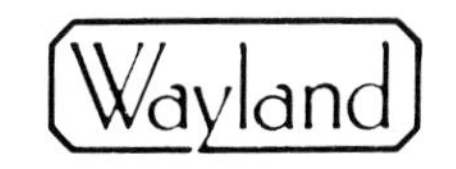

Healthy Living

Healthy Teeth
Healthy Hair
Healthy Skin
Healthy Eyes
Healthy Hands and Feet
Healthy Eating

Words printed in **bold** are explained in the glossary

First Published in 1990 by
Wayland Publishers Limited
61 Western Road, Hove
East Sussex, BN3 1JD, England

Consultant: Diana Bentley, Reading
Consultant, University of Reading
Editor: James Kerr

British Library Cataloguing in Publication Data
Milburn, Constance
Healthy hands and feet.
1. Man. Hands. Feet. Beauty care
I. Title II. Series
646.727

ISBN 1-85210-930-0

Typeset by N. Taylor, Wayland Publishers Limited
Printed and bound by Casterman S.A., Belgium

Contents

Why we need healthy hands and feet	4
Using our hands	6
Keeping hands clean	8
Looking after hands	10
Problems for hands	12
Looking after nails	14
Keeping feet clean	16
Looking after feet	18
Buying a new pair of shoes	20
Wearing the correct shoes	22
Problems for feet	24
Help from the chiropodist	26
Standing and walking correctly	28
Glossary	30
Books to read	31
Index	32

Why we need healthy hands and feet

All day long we use our hands and feet. We use our hands for holding and touching and our feet for standing and walking.

Make a list of all the other things we use our hands and feet for – you will be surprised to see how long the list is!

We must make sure our hands and feet stay healthy because they are so important to us. This means we must look after them carefully, keep them clean and dry, and wear well-fitting shoes.

Using our hands

We use our hands in all sorts of ways. We can grip, squeeze, twist, push, pull, wave and throw with our hands. Were all these on your list? Could you eat an apple, write a letter, or throw a ball without the use of your hands? It would be very difficult.

We also use our hands for touching. Touching things can actually stop us from hurting ourselves badly. When you touch something very sharp or hot, you feel pain. The pain makes you quickly take your hand away so that it is safe.

Keeping hands clean

Hands need to be washed regularly because they are used such a lot. When washing your hands, you should cover them with warm water and soap, rub them together and then rinse them under clean water. If there is any dirt under your fingernails, you need to use a nailbrush to remove it.

It is very important to wash your hands:

- before touching or eating food.
- after going to the toilet.
- after painting, or doing any other messy work.

- after handling dirty objects.
- before or after touching a cut or graze.
- after playing with pets, or touching animals.

There are lots of other times when your hands get dirty. Always remember to wash your hands whenever they are dirty.

Looking after hands

Here are some good ways of looking after hands:

- drying them thoroughly after washing. This is because damp skin can become sore and **chapped**.

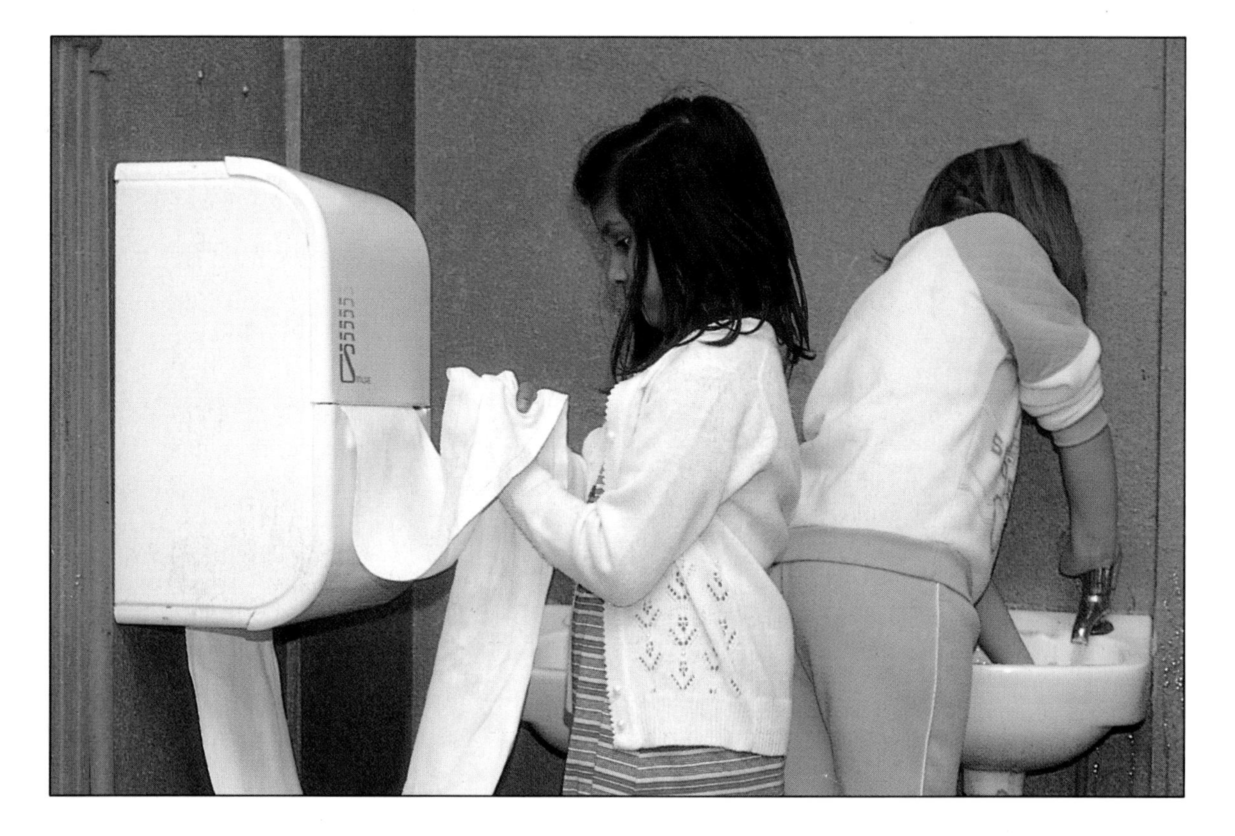

- keeping them warm. Remember to wear gloves in very cold weather. Gloves also stop your hands from becoming chapped.

Hands can be damaged by:

- being burnt. This can happen if you touch something too hot, like a kettle, cooker or lighted match.
- being cut. This can happen if you are careless when you are using a knife, or when there are pieces of broken glass about.

- becoming **infected**. This can happen if dirt gets into a small cut or if you write on your hands with a ballpoint pen or ink. The chemicals can enter the skin and cause an infection.

Problems for hands

Cuts:
Hands are so busy that they can easily be damaged accidentally. If you cut your hand, you should wash the open **wound** straight away. Then cover it with a bandage to keep dirt out, otherwise the wound can become infected.

Warts:

These are small, hard lumps of skin that sometimes grow on your hands and fingers. Although warts don't look very nice, they are not painful.

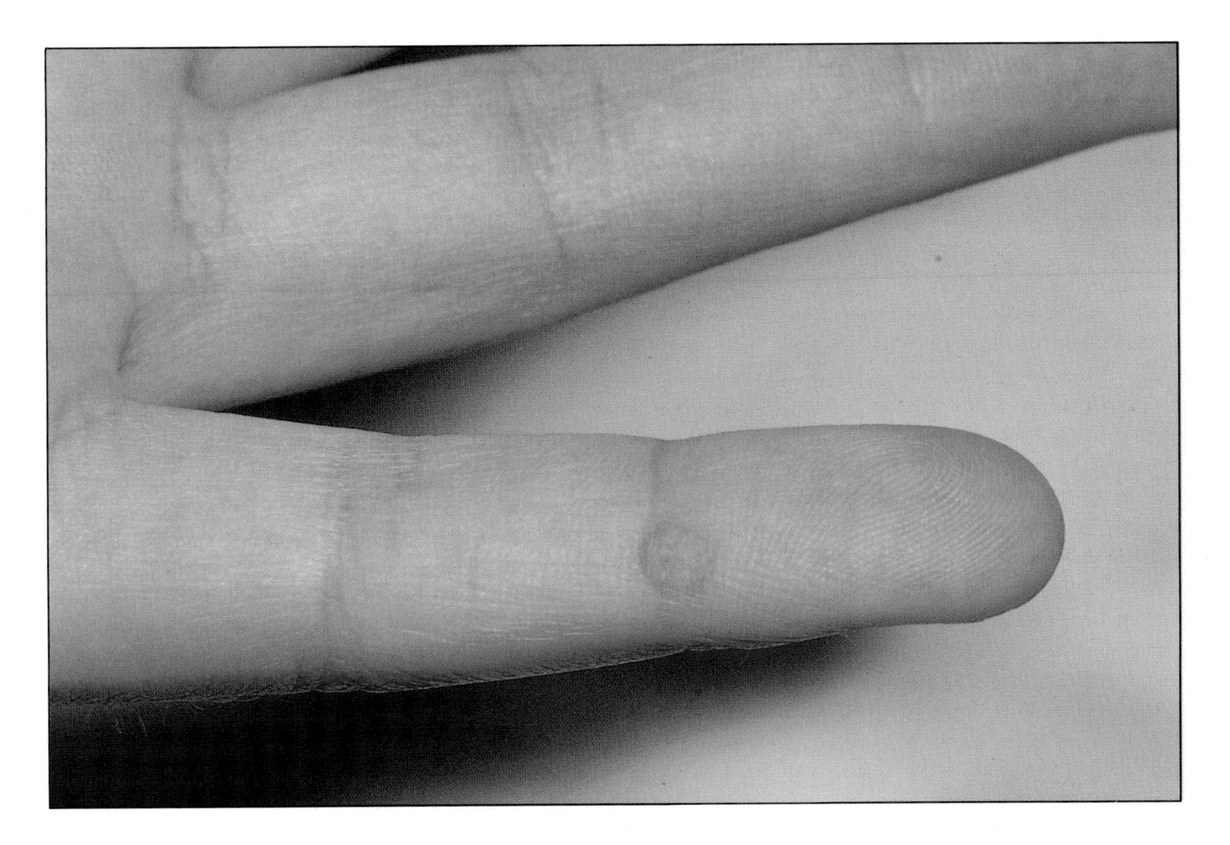

Chilblains:

Chilblains can occur if your hands are very cold and you try to warm them up too quickly. Rub them first, to warm them up. Then you can put them in front of a radiator or near a fire.

Looking after nails

Your nails are growing all the time, so they need to be cut frequently. This can be done with a pair of nail scissors or **clippers**.

It is much easier to cut your nails after you have had a bath, because water softens them. Fingernails should be cut in a curve that matches the shape of your finger, but toenails should be cut straight across.

The top corners of toenails can sometimes grow into the skin of the toes. These are called ingrowing toenails and they can be very painful. Cutting your toenails straight across helps to prevent ingrowing toenails.

Some people like to bite their nails. However, this is a very unhealthy habit. If you bite your nails, you might swallow dirt, which would make you ill. Also, bitten-down nails do not look very nice!

Keeping feet clean

Feet should be washed every day, because they can get sweaty. Sweaty feet feel sticky and smell nasty! Dirt often sticks in between the toes and on the backs of the ankles, so make sure you wash these parts thoroughly.

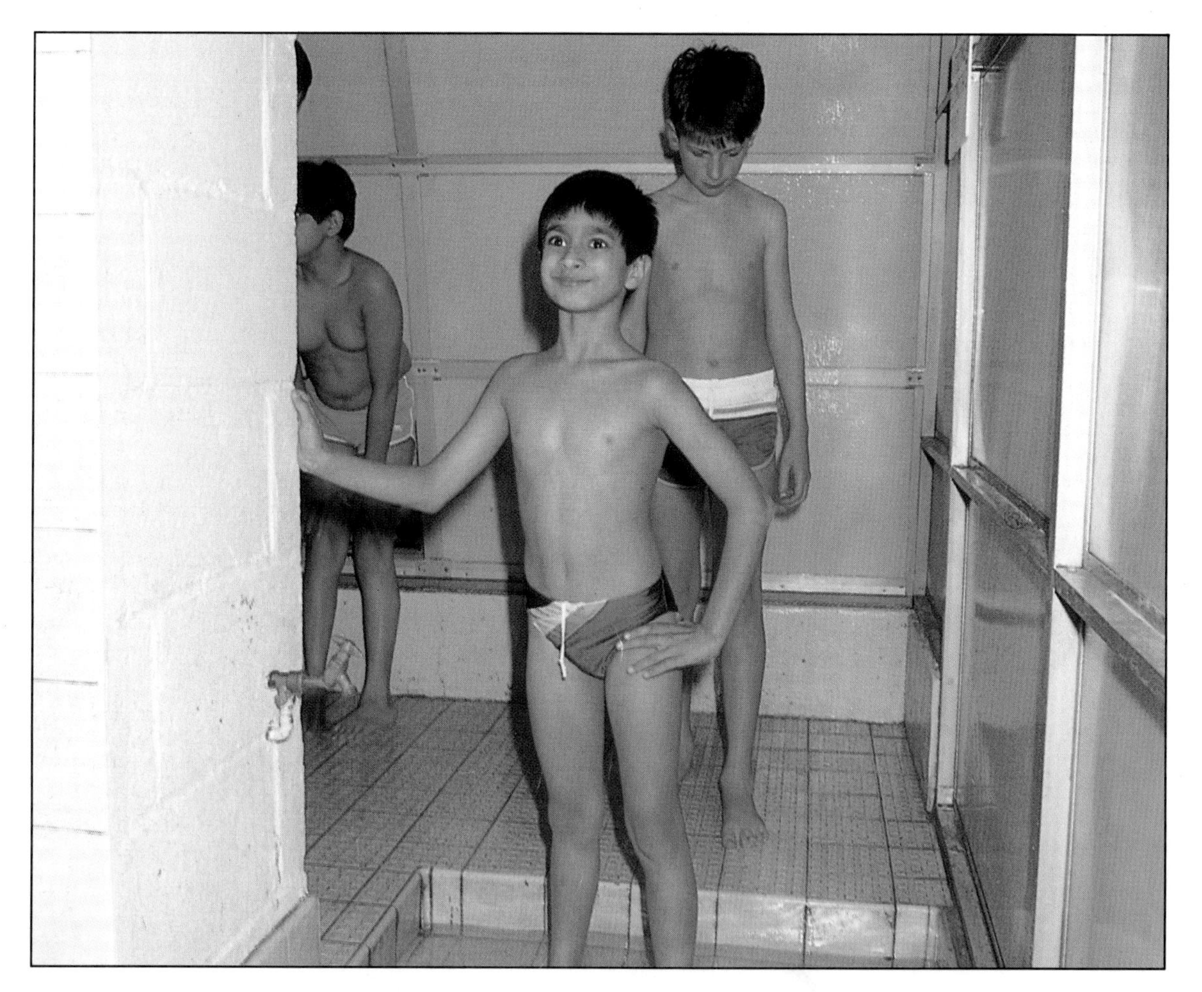

Drying your feet well, after you have washed them, is important too. You should rub them briskly with a towel, to remove any dead skin.

Drying in between your toes is especially important. This is because damp skin between the toes can easily become sore and infected. Sprinkle your feet with talcum powder, to make them completely dry. This also makes it easier to put your socks on!

Looking after feet

Your feet are growing fast. This means they can easily be damaged by wearing socks or shoes that are too small. If your feet do not have room to grow, the bones may not grow straight. It is not a good idea to wear shoes that someone else has worn, because they won't be the same shape as your feet.

Try not to run about without your shoes on. You might tread on a **splinter**, a sharp stone or a piece of glass or metal, and hurt your feet.

If ever your feet get very cold, do not warm them on a hot-water bottle or in front of a radiator straight away. This is because you can get chilblains on your feet as well as your hands.

Buying a new pair of shoes

The reason we wear shoes is to protect and support our feet. It is very important that shoes should fit properly. When you go to buy a new pair of shoes, the shop assistant will probably measure your feet. It is important to know what size of shoes will fit you most comfortably.

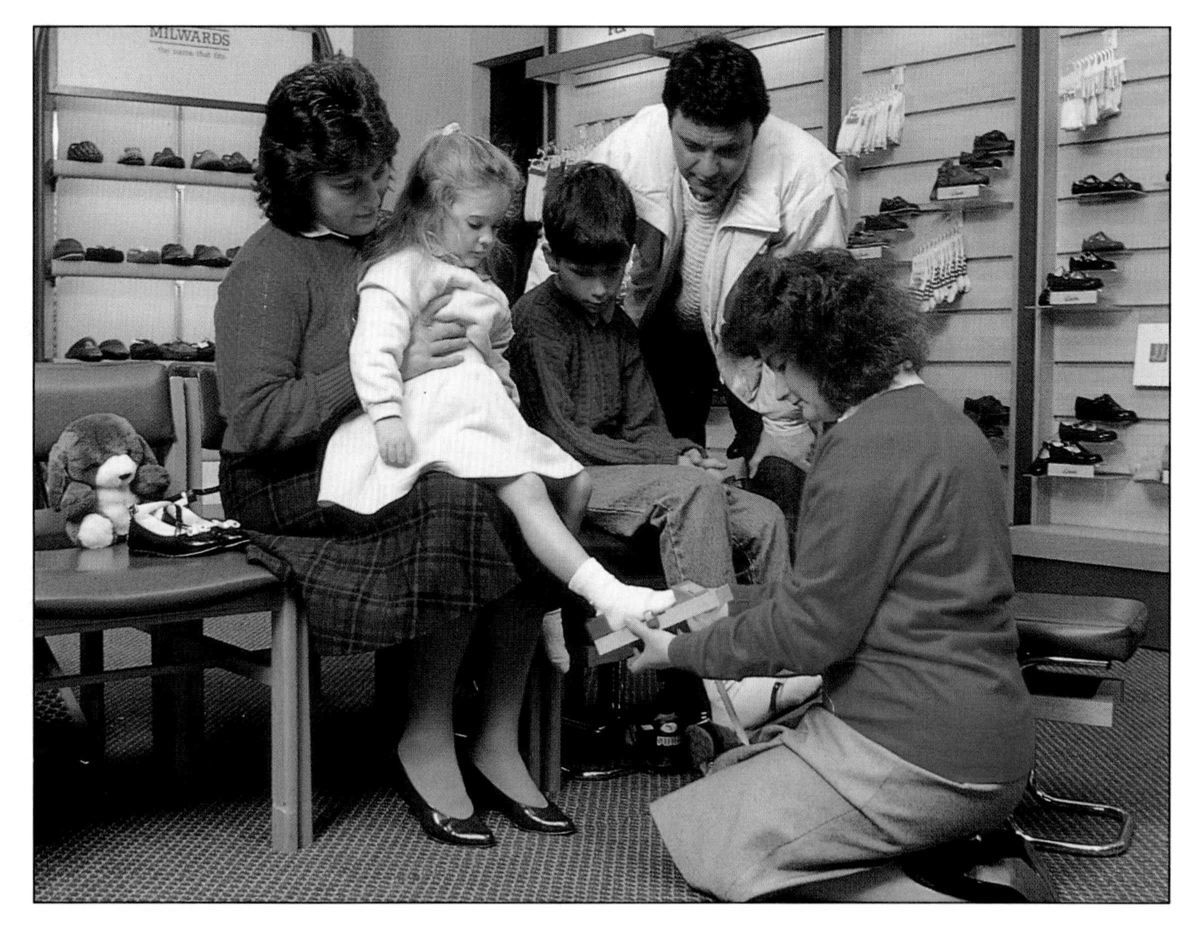

When you try on a new pair of shoes, stand up and walk around in them. They should fit snugly around your heels and you should be able to wiggle your toes. New shoes should feel comfortable the first time you put them on. If they don't feel comfortable, don't buy them.

Wearing the correct shoes

We have to wear special shoes for some activities. This is because our feet need support and protection in different ways, depending on what we are doing.

School shoes should be flat, **flexible**, comfortable and strong. It is a good idea to wear training shoes for outside games.

There are special shoes for some sports. Footballers wear boots with studs in them. These shoes grip the football pitch much better than shoes with flat **soles**. Different types of dancing, such as tap and ballet, need special shoes.

High-heeled shoes and slip-on shoes may look nice, but they should only be worn on special occasions, and not every day. This is because they do not give proper support to our feet.

Wellington boots were made to protect our feet from rain and mud. **Hikers** have special walking shoes which give extra support to their ankles.

Verrucas:

Verrucas look like tiny black spots, but they can get bigger if they are not treated. They are really warts which grow on feet and they can be very painful.

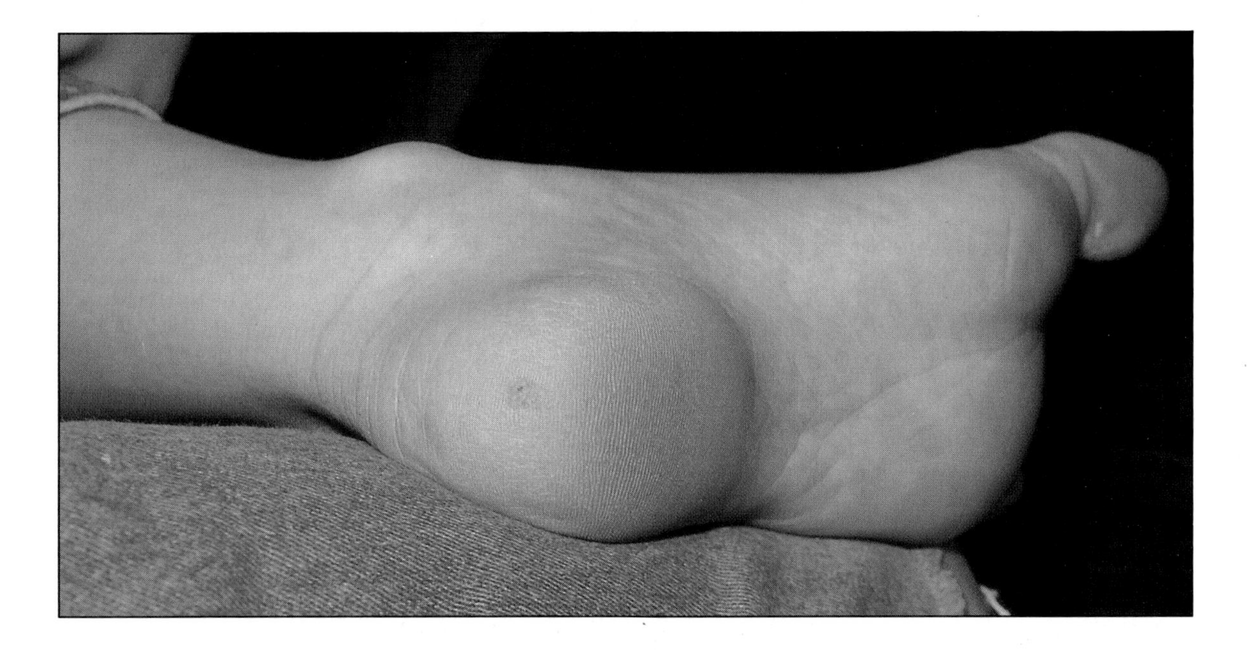

Verrucas can be passed on between people. You can catch them by walking barefoot where someone with verrucas has walked. It is easy to catch verrucas in changing rooms at schools or sports centres, where many people walk barefoot. Some people think that it is a good idea to wear something on your feet in changing rooms.

Try to check the bottoms of your feet every day, to make sure that you do not have any verrucas. If you do find one, never go barefoot until it has been treated. Verrucas can be treated at the school clinic, or by a doctor.

Athlete's foot:

Athlete's foot is an infection which usually starts between the toes. The skin becomes itchy and red, and begins to peel. If you get athlete's foot, you should visit the doctor for treatment.

Help from the chiropodist

A person who looks after people's feet is called a **chiropodist**. If you have any foot problems, you can visit a chiropodist.

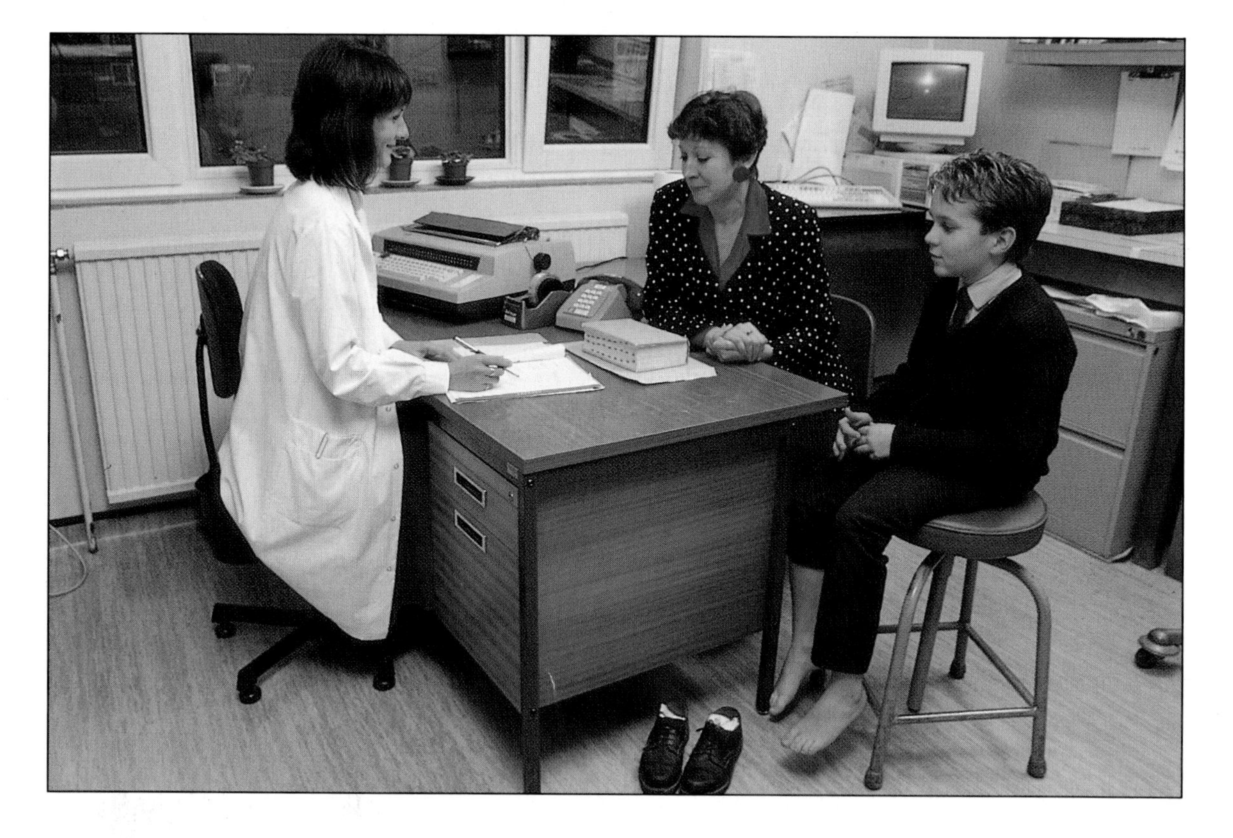

Chiropodists can often help with walking problems. Some children walk with their heels leaning over to one side. Some walk with their toes turned inwards. Problems like these need to be corrected while the bones in the feet are still growing.

Chiropodists will give advice about what needs to be done. They might suggest special foot-exercises or that the shoes should be built up on one side.

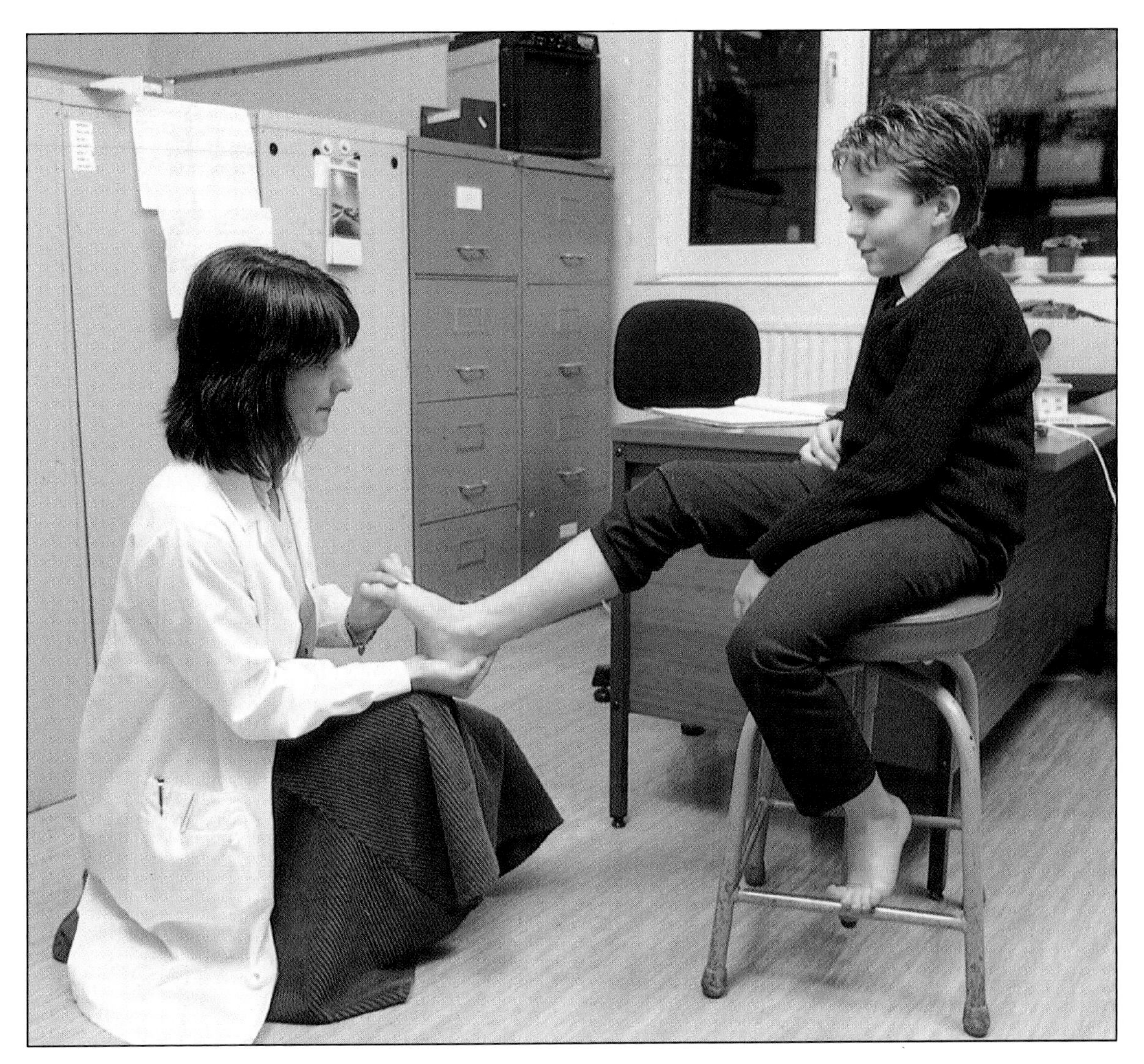

Standing and walking correctly

Did you know that your feet support your whole body-weight? In fact, they support your body-weight all your life. You only rest them when you are sitting or lying down!

To be healthy and active, you need to have good **posture**. This means that when you are standing upright, your head should be balanced directly on top of your **spine**. You should be able to feel your weight passing straight down your body, through your spine, hips and legs, and finally to your feet.

To be able to balance properly and support your body-weight, you need to have strong, healthy feet and wear comfortable, well-fitting shoes.

Glossary

Athlete's foot An infection of the skin of the foot.
Chapped Cracked and rough skin, caused by cold weather.
Chilblains Sore patches, or swellings, on the skin.
Chiropodist A person whose job it is to look after other people's feet.
Clippers A tool for cutting or trimming nails.
Flexible Able to bend easily.
Hikers People who go for long walks in the countryside.
Infected Diseased.
Posture The way a person holds his or her body when standing, sitting or walking.
Soles The bottoms of feet or shoes.
Spine The backbone.
Splinter A small, thin, sharp piece of wood, glass or other hard material.
Verrucas Warts on the feet.
Wound A scratch, or cut, on the skin.

Books to read

Body Facts by Dr. Alan Maryon Davis (Macdonald, 1984).
Health and Hygiene by Dorothy Baldwin (Wayland, 1987).
My Hands by Susan Baker (Macdonald, 1983).
Touch by Ed Catherall (Wayland, 1982).
Touch, Taste and Smell by Steve Parker (Franklin Watts, 1989).
Your Hands and Feet by Joan Iveson-Iveson (Wayland, 1985).

Picture acknowledgements

All photographs by Trevor Hill except *cover* ZEFA.

Index

Ankles 16, 23
Athlete's foot 25

Ballet shoes 23
Bones 18, 27

Chapped skin 10
Chilblains 13, 19
Chiropodist 26–7
Cuts 9, 11, 12

Drying 5, 10, 17

Fingers 13, 15
Football boots 23

Gloves 10

Heels 21, 26
Holding 4

Infection 11, 12, 17
Ingrowing toenails 15

Nailbrush 8
Nails 8, 14–15
  fingernails 8, 15
  toenails 15
Nail scissors 14

Shoes 5, 18, 20–21, 22–3, 27, 29
Skin 10, 11, 13, 15, 17
Socks 17, 18
Standing 4, 7, 21, 28–9

Talcum powder 17
Toes 16, 17, 21, 26
Touching 4, 9, 11
Training shoes 22

Verrucas 24, 25

Walking 4, 21, 23, 24, 26, 28–9
Warts 13, 24
Washing 8, 9, 10, 12, 16, 17
Wellington boots 23